beautiful knits for heads, hands and toes

beautiful KNITS

for heads, hands and toes

stunning accessories for you to knit

ALISON DUPERNEX

NEW HOLLAND

First published in 2008 by New Holland Publishers (UK) Ltd
London · Cape Town · Sydney · Auckland

Garfield House, 86-88 Edgware Road, London W2 2EA,
United Kingdom
www.newhollandpublishers.com

80 McKenzie Street, Cape Town 8001, South Africa
Unit 1, 66 Gibbes Street, Chatswood, NSW 2067, Australia
218 Lake Road, Northcote, Auckland, New Zealand

ISBN 978 1 84773 119 7

Senior Editor: Emma Pattison
Production: Marion Storz
Design: bluegumdesigners.com
Photography: Paul Bricknell
Styling: Susie Johns
Illustrations: Carrie Hill
Stitch Diagrams: Kuo Kang Chen
Pattern checking: Sue Horan
Editorial Direction: Rosemary Wilkinson

10 9 8 7 6 5 4 3 2 1

Reproduction by Colourscan Overseas Co Pte Ltd, Singapore
Printed and bound by Craft Print International Ltd, Singapore

contents

introduction

Knitting is so versatile. With just a minimum of equipment (two sticks and some yarn) you can fashion hats, gloves, bags, socks, clothing, jewellery, and in fact almost anything.

Knitting is relaxing, and as you become familiar with your pattern your work develops a rhythm – needle in, yarn round, draw through and repeat – which can be totally absorbing. You can also knit while watching the television, so you feel you are not wasting time!

I encourage you to experiment with the colours, yarn, or size of these projects and make them your own. Knit some flowers with big wool and needles to embellish slippers, bags or scarves, or try felting the projects. Although the size of the slippers, socks or gloves is important it does not really matter if a bag, scarf or brooch is a few centimetres longer or shorter. If in doubt make a small test piece before embarking on the full design (several test pieces can be sewn together to make a cushion cover so they won't go to waste). Use squared paper (1 square = 1 stitch) to design your own intarsia or Fairisle projects, or add pompoms or tassels to personalise.

Knitting is so portable, you can take it with you wherever you go. Knit with friends, on the train, in the pub, on the beach, in your lunch break, and any time you are waiting for someone or something. Enjoy!

Alison Dupernex

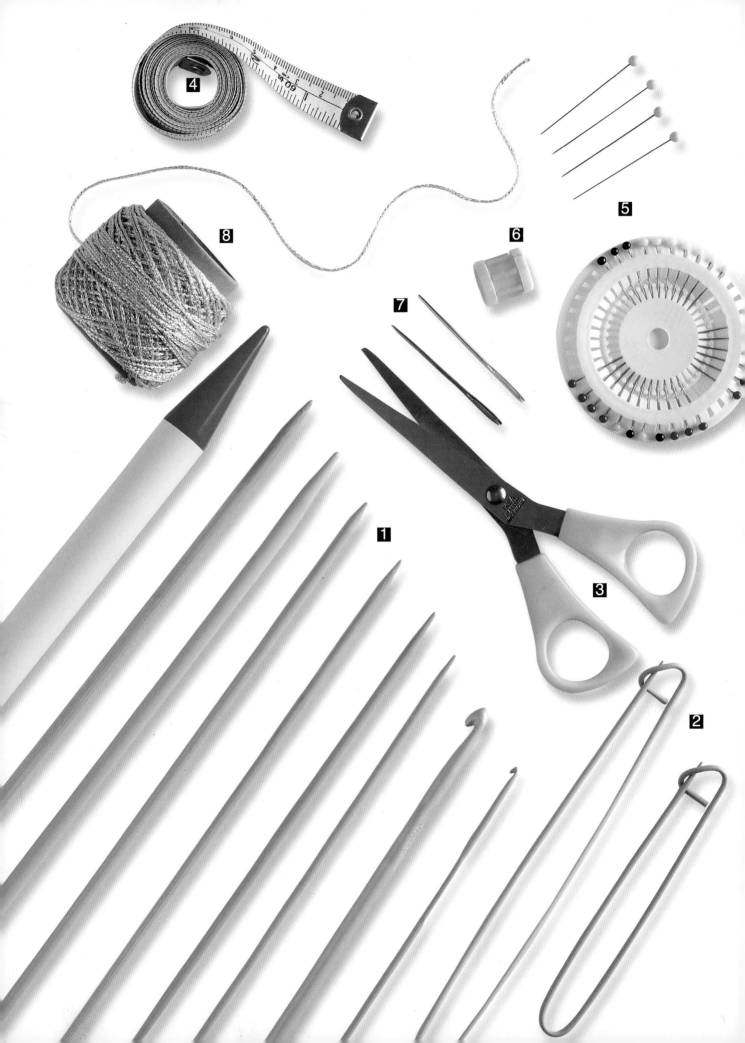

equipment

Two needles and some yarn are all the materials you need to begin knitting, but here are some accessories which will make life easier. Do not be tempted to use old or damaged needles which can be found in charity shops or attics, as they may be bent or chipped and will snag your yarn. Besides, there is nothing nicer than a brand new set of tools. There are a wide variety of yarns available – fluffy, stringy, random dyed, luxurious silk, cashmere, alpaca or wool – and the type of yarn you choose will determine the look of your finished accessory. Choose a yarn you like the feel of in a colour you love and your chosen project will be a joy to work.

Knitting needles (1)

These are available in plastic, metal or bamboo. The yarn slides off plastic needles easier but if you are using fine yarn and loose stitches bamboo grips a little better and you are less likely to drop stitches.

Double-pointed needles (2)

Several of the patterns are made using these needles which have points at both ends. The stitches are divided fairly evenly over three of four needles with the last needle being used to knit the stitches. You must make sure that you keep an even tension especially when transferring from one needle to the next. To help when casting on, cast on the required number of sts on the first needle, and an extra one, then slip this last st onto the next needle and continue to cast on.

Scissors (3)

Round ended scissors are best. Never use your knitting scissors to cut paper or for any other purpose or the blades will blunt.

Tape measure (4)

Essential for measuring tension squares and knitting.

Pins (5)

I use brightly coloured glass headed pins as they are easy to see and will not be left in your work by mistake.

Stitch holder (6)

Used to hold stitches which you are not working on at the time.

Tapestry and darning needles (7)

Have a supply in different sizes for different thicknesses of yarn.

Yarns (8)

All of the projects in this book have recommended yarn types but the yarn can be substituted with care. Be sure that the replacement yarn is of the same weight, yardage, and fibre content and check that the tension is the same as the recommended yarn. The yarn label will provide you with all this information. Always buy enough yarn as different dye lots can vary considerably.

Knitting needle conversion table

Metric	British	American
2 mm	14	00
2¼ mm	13	1
2¾ mm	12	2
3 mm	11	n/a
3¼ mm	10	3
3¾ mm	9	5
4 mm	8	6
4½ mm	7	7
5 mm	6	8
5½ mm	5	9
6 mm	4	10
6½ mm	3	10½
7 mm	2	n/a
7½ mm	1	n/a
8 mm	0	11
9 mm	00	13
10 mm	000	15

techniques

Knitted fabric is made by looping a continuous length of yarn with the aid of two needles interlocking another loop through the first. The versatile fabric produced is elastic, warm and durable. There are 4 basic techniques – the cast on, the knit stitch, the purl stitch and the cast off. All knitting patterns are based on these simple techniques.

getting started

With your new needles, some chosen yarn and a knitting pattern, sit comfortably and with a little practice you will soon get into a rhythm. Always remember to avoid knitting with hot hands as your tension will be uneven. All knitting must begin by casting on – this is the action of putting stitches onto your needle and is the basis of all the knitting you will ever do.

Tension

This is the number of stitches and rows to a certain measurement. Always check your tension, as a variation from the pattern can make a substantial difference to the size of your finished project and the amount of yarn used. Knit a square at least 15 cm

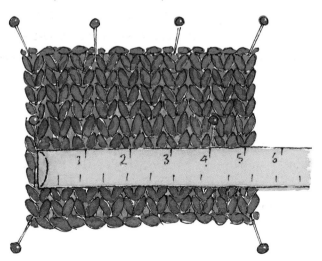

(6 ins). Measure a 10 cm (4 in) square in centre and mark with pins. Count how many stitches and rows are inside the marked square. If there are more than recommended change to larger needles and if too few, change to smaller needles.

Cast on

These are the two most useful methods for casting on – the Thumb Method and the Cable Cast On.

Thumb method

Make a slip knot on the right hand needle allowing yourself plenty of yarn as a tail, wind this around your left thumb front to back, insert the needle along the thumb into the loop. Using your right hand wrap the yarn from the ball over the needle. Pull the yarn through the loop to make a stitch and tighten by pulling gently on the tail end. Repeat for more sts.

Cable cast on

Make a slip knot on the left hand needle, insert the right hand needle from front to back through the loop, wrap the yarn around the right hand needle, keeping the needle tip up draw the needle through the loop to make a new stitch. Slip this new stitch from the right needle onto the left. * Insert the right needle between these 2 sts and wrap the yarn around the needle and pull through to make another st. Place onto the left hand needle. Repeat from * between the last two sts until you have achieved the required amount. Note: Leave a good length of tail to use when sewing up.

the stitches

The first stitch to learn is the knit stitch. The purl stitch is the reverse of the knit stitch. Once you have mastered these 2 stitches you will be able to knit hundreds of different variations of these basic stitches and follow many knitting patterns.

Garter stitch

The knit stitch and purl stitch are fundamental to knitting and both are easy to learn.

Knit stitch

This really is the keystone stitch. All other stitches are variations of this technique. With the cast on stitch needle in your left hand, insert the point of the right hand needle in the front of the first stitch. Holding the yarn in your right hand take it under the right needle and between the needles, then using the point of the right needle pick up the yarn between the two needles and pull it through making a loop, at the same time lift the stitch off the left needle. This is one worked stitch. Repeat to complete the row.

Purl stitch

To purl a stitch, insert the right needle in the first stitch on the left needle with the point and yarn at the front of the work. Take the yarn and loop it around the right needle, draw the loop through the stitch on the left needle and complete by slipping the stitch off the left. Repeat this method across the row.

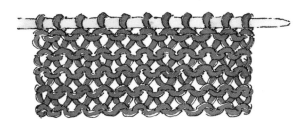

Stocking stitch

This is made by knitting one row of knit stitch and one row of purl stitch. One side will be smooth, usually referred to as the right side, and the other side will be ridged. If the ridged side is used as the right side this is reverse stocking stitch.

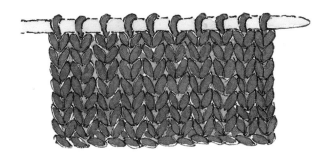

shaping & finishing

Some projects require shaping and this is achieved by either increasing or decreasing as you knit. In some patterns the method used is specified, in others a simple instruction to increase or decrease is given. Take time to make your shaping as neat as possible as it will affect the quality of your work.

Increasing and decreasing

Increasing or decreasing is essential for shaping necks, sleeve edges, bag fronts and socks. There are several ways of achieving this but the main methods you will use are described below.

Increase

Insert the right hand needle into the front of the stitch and knit it but do not take it off the needle, insert the same needle into the back of the same stitch and knit it. Slip stitches off the left needle.

Make 1 Increase

Insert the right hand needle into the stitch on the left hand needle but one row down. Knit the stitch in the usual way. This makes an almost invisible increase.

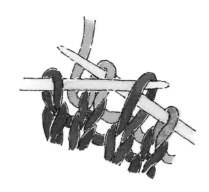

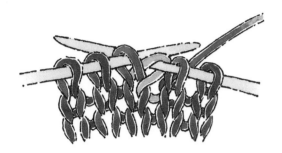

Decrease

A very simple decrease is to knit 2 stitches together. Insert the right hand needle from left to right through the next 2 stitches and knit them together.

Slip stitch decrease

Another method used in the projects is Slip one, Knit 1, Pass Slipped Stitch Over (sl1, K1, psso). Insert the right hand needle into the next stitch on the left hand needle and slip it onto the right (sl1), knit the next stitch (K1), then insert the left hand needle into the slipped stitch and lift it over the knitted stitch and off the right hand needle (psso).

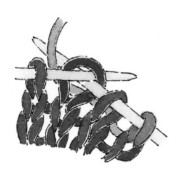

Picking up stitches

This technique is used when you need to knit directly onto another piece of knitting, either along a straight seam or shaped edge. With the right side facing, insert the knitting needle from front to back between the first and second stitches of the edge, wrap the yarn around the needle and use the point of the needle to pull the yarn through to the right side of the work and a stitch will have been formed. Continue in this way along the edge until the required number of stitches has been picked up.

Casting off (binding off)

When you have completed your piece of work it must be finished off to prevent the stitches unravelling. It is essential not to cast off too tightly, sometimes a larger needle can be used to prevent this. Knit 2 stitches, insert the point of the left needle into the first stitch and lift it up and drop it over the second stitch. Knit the next stitch and repeat the process until all the stitches have been cast off. Cut the yarn and thread through the last loop and pull gently to close. Casting off in pattern simply means, work the stitch as it should be according to the pattern and lift it over as before.

Finishing off

Spend time finishing off your work. There is little point taking time knitting a project only to rush sewing up and finishing. The most useful methods for joining pieces are mattress stitch and back stitch.

Mattress stitch

This produces an almost invisible seam. With right sides facing and side by side thread a tapestry needle with yarn and secure to the lower right corner by over sewing. Take the needle across to the left edge and under the strand of yarn between the first and second stitches of the first row. Next take the needle back to the opposite edge and insert it one row up, between the first and second stitches of the row. Repeat this process moving up the seam. When a few stitches have been completed gently pull the yarn up to close the gap. Do not pull too tightly or the seam will pucker, allow some elasticity.

Back stitch

With right sides of the work together one on top of the other, secure the sewing yarn to the base of the seam and working one stitch in from the edge, take the tapestry needle down through both pieces of work and come out two rows to the left. Next take the needle to the right and insert it where the previous stitch ended, take it behind the work to emerge four rows to the left, pull the yarn gently to finish off the stitch and repeat this process along the seam.

changing colour

The yarn colours you choose are fundamental to the success of the finished piece and the ability to change colour while knitting is very important. Why not be creative and vary the colours of a project to suit your own style? The two methods for changing colour, fairisle and intarsia, are explained below.

Fairisle knitting

True Fairisle has no more than 2 colours in a row although with the intricacy of many of the designs it may look more than that. There are two ways to keep your colours neat at the back of your work and the first is stranding. When you change colour over a short distance, about 5 stitches, just pick up the second colour making sure that it is not tight across the back of the work and start to work to the next colour change. Then pick up the other colour and continue. The other method is knitting-in where the second colour is caught up and almost woven into the back. With the colour being used in the right hand and the second colour in your left bring it over the right needle and knit the stitch with the main colour, bringing it under the other yarn. It will then go under the next stitch. Knit the next stitch and repeat the instructions again and the second colour is caught up in every other stitch.

Intarsia

If you are working large blocks of colour as in Rosy Cape and Bag the intarsia technique is used. When there is a colour change twist the two yarns around each other where they meet on the wrong side to prevent a hole. The yarn ends can be knitted-in as each colour joins. To prevent a big knot of yarns at the back of your work use 1–2 m (1–2 yards) lengths of yarn.

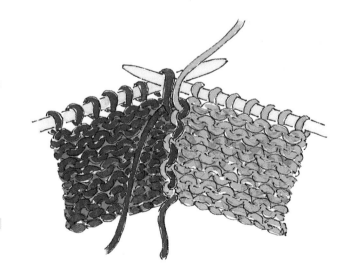

working from charts

Colour charts

Some Fairisle and intarsia projects are shown on a colour chart. Each square represents a stitch and a colour. The first row is at the bottom and you work up to the top row. If the design is repeated as in the Fairisle patterns the width of the chart is knitted and then start back at the beginning. There is a key which denotes which symbol corresponds to which shade and yarn type.

Symbol charts

These are often used with cable projects. Each square denotes a stitch pattern shown on the accompanying key.

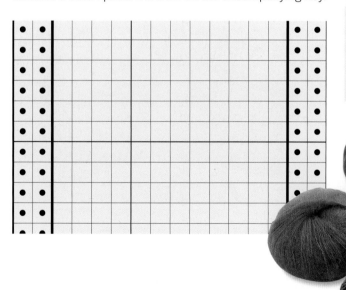

Glossary

Cast off, bind off	Used when you have finished your knitting. Knit 2 sts then * lift the 1st stitch over the second, knit the next stitch and repeat from *.
Cast on	Before you can start knitting you need some stitches on your needle and the rest of your work will continue on this foundation row.
Decrease	Reduce the number of stitches in a row by working stitches together.
Increase	Add stitches in a row by knitting into the front and back of a stitch or M1 by picking up a stitch from the previous row or yo which makes a hole and can be decorative.
Knitwise	Insert the needle into the stitch as if you were about to knit it.
Pick up and knit	Insert the needle into the loops along the edge and knit it as a stitch – as in sock gusset.
With RS facing	The right side of the work must be facing you and the wrong side away from you, usually when shaping or starting to pattern.

techniques

Abbreviations

alt	alternate	P	purl
beg	beginning	patt	pattern
MB	make bobble	psso	pass slip stitch over
cm	centimetres	P2 tog	purl 2 together
cont	continue	rem	remaining
dec	decrease	rep	repeat
DK	double knitting	RS	right side
foll	following	sl	slip
g	gram	st(s)	stitch(es)
g st	garter stitch, all rows are knit	st st	stocking stitch
ins	inches	tbl	through back of loop
inc	increase	tog	together
K	knit	WS	wrong side
kfb	knit into front and back of a st	yf	yarn forward
Ktbl	Knit into back loop of st	yo	yarn over needle
K2 tog	knit two together	yo twice	yarn over twice
M	main colour		

bright & beautiful

Sugar pink, dove grey and denim blue with a splash of ochre make an alchemy of colours to suit any outfit. Zingy chevrons in French navy, lemon, chocolate, bilberry, olive, stone, lime and shades of delphinium will brighten up a cloudy day, or why not warm yourself with scarlet and mullberry.

country scarf

This warm and cosy scarf can be made in a weekend. The chunky yarn and large needles make short work of this project. Have a go at making the textured stripes deeper or change to a different colour for each stripe. Keep the design simple or jazz it up with red or blue yarns.

measurements
Width: 27 cm (10½ in)
Length: 158 cm (62 in)

materials
6 x 50 g balls Rowan Country in Birch 650
Pair 7½ mm (US 10½) knitting needles
Darning needle

tension
11 sts and 16 rows to 10 cm (4 in) measured over patt using 7½ mm (US 10½) needles.

abbreviations
See page 15.

note
■ The stitch pattern is inclined to concertina so pull the scarf out firmly to measure the length.

scarf
Cast on 30 sts.
1st row: K.
2nd row: P.
3rd to 8th rows: Rep 1st and 2nd rows 3 times.
9th row: K.

These 9 rows form patt.
Cont in patt until scarf measures 158 cm (62 in) ending with a 9th patt row.
Cast off.
Sew in all ends and press lightly.

bright & beautiful

country hat

Knit this snuggly hat in the same colourway as the Country Scarf to make a perfect pair, or wear it alone with a chunky jumper to keep you warm on a cold day. Either way you can have lots of fun by experimenting with different coloured yarns, and the pattern is so simple you may find yourself knitting several!

measurement
Circumference: 50 cm (20 in)

materials
2 x 50 g balls Rowan Country in Birch 650
Pair 7½ mm (US 10½) knitting needles
Darning needle

tension
11 sts and 16 rows to 10 cm (4 in) measured over patt using 7½ mm (US 10½) needles.

abbreviations
See page 15.

note
■ You may want to use a different yarn to sew the hat up as the yarn used to knit this pattern has a tendency to pull apart as it's being sewn.

hat
Cast on 55 sts.
1st row: K.
2nd row: P.
3rd row: K.
4th row: P.
5th row: K.
These 5 rows form patt.
Rep 1st to 5th rows 3 times more.

crown shaping
1st row: [Patt 4, patt 2 tog] to last st, patt 1. (46 sts)
Patt 4 rows.
6th row: [Patt 2, patt 2 tog] to last 2 sts, patt 2. (35 sts)
Patt 4 rows.
11th row: [Patt 1, patt 2 tog] to last 2 sts, patt 2. (24 sts).
Patt 4 rows.
16th row: [Patt 2 tog] to end. (12 sts).
Patt 3 rows.
20th row: [Patt 2 tog] to end. (6 sts).

to make up
Break yarn and thread through rem sts and draw up. Sew back seam.

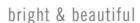
bright & beautiful

country bucket bag

This bag will carry everything you need, including the kitchen sink! It looks huge when knitted but shrinks when felted. Using large needles and thick wool, it really won't take long to knit. Add another pocket or make the handle longer, but remember you will need to be able to carry it when full.

measurements
after felting:
Side seam to base: 29 cm (11½ in)
Circumference: 100 cm (39¼ in)

materials
12 x 50g balls Rowan Country in Juniper 654
Pair 7 mm (US 10½) knitting needles
2 large buttons
Darning needle

tension
12 sts and 17 rows to 10 cm (4 in), before felting, over st st using 7 mm (US 10½) needles.

abbreviations
See page 15.

notes
■ Knit 2 tension squares and wash one in the machine to ascertain how firm you want your bag when felted.
■ Use natural buttons with natural yarns – chose shell or wood to enhance and embelish the bag.

base
Cast on 10 sts. Work in st st throughout.
K 1 row.
Inc 1 st at the beg of every row until there are 28 sts.
Cont straight until Base measures 35 cm (13¾ in).
Dec 1 st at beg of every row until 10 sts rem.
Work 1 row.
Cast off.
Mark centre of the cast-on and cast-off edges with coloured thread.

bright & beautiful

The fully fashioned decreasing makes a neat edge to the handle on this fun bag.

back

With RS of Base facing, and beg at one marker, pick up and K 60 sts evenly around edge of base to 2nd marker.

Beg with a P row, work in st st until Back measures 46 cm (18 in), ending with a P row.

handle shaping

Next row: K1, s11, K1, psso, K to last 3 sts, K2tog, K1.

Next row: P.

Rep these 2 rows until 20 sts rem. Cont straight until Back measures 95 cm (37½ in) from the Base.

Cast off.

Work Front to match.

pocket

Cast on 30 sts and st st 40 rows. Cast off.

bright & beautiful

to make up

Join side seams to start of handle shaping. Overlap the handle ends by 2.5 cm (1 in) and stitch together. Place pocket on Front and sew sides and base. Make 2 loops and stitch one on Front just above centre of pocket and 2nd at top of one side seam. Make sure they are large enough for the button allowing for 2 cm (1 in) shrinkage when washed. Darn in all ends. Place the bag with a towel in a washing machine and wash at 60° through a full cycle. It may need to be washed again if you require more felting – it is not an exact science. Sew one button on pocket and 2nd at top of opposite side seam to button loop.

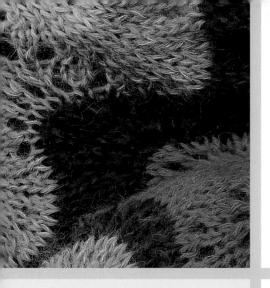

feather & fan wrap

Knit a classic wrap in a lacy, traditional Shetland pattern. Wave upon wave of lace and purl rows make this look complicated, but it is so easy and very effective with a pretty scalloped edging. Try sewing seed pearl beads on the ends for a glamorous look, or maybe add a fringe.

measurements
Width: 66 cm (26 in)
Length: 176 cm (69 in)

materials
1 x 50 g ball Rowan Kid Classic in each of Frilly 844 (A), Victoria 852 (B), Lavender Ice 841 (C), Crystal 840 (D), Glacier 822 (E), Feather 828 (F) and Royal 835 (G)
Pair 7 mm (US 10½) knitting needles
Darning needle

tension
18 sts and 17½ rows to 11 cm (4¼ in) measured over Feather and Fan patt using 7 mm (US 10½) needles.

abbreviations
See page 15.

notes
■ When changing yarn at the beginning of a row knit in both ends for several stitches for a neater finish.

feather and fan patt
(multiple of 18 sts)
1st row (RS): K.
2nd row: P.
3rd row: * (K2tog) 3 times, (yo, K1) 6 times, (K2tog) 3 times, rep from * to end.
4th row: P.
These 4 rows form Feather and Fan patt.

wrap
Using 7 mm (US 10½) needles and A, cast on 108 sts.
* Cont in Feather and Fan patt joining in at beg and fastening off at end of each stripe. Work 4 rows each A, B, C, D, E, F and G. *
** Patt 8 rows each A, B, C, D, E, F and G. **
Rep from ** to ** 3 times more.
Rep from * to * once.
Cast off in G.

to make up
Darn in ends. Press according to instructions on yarn label.

bright & beautiful

reflection chevron bag

So called because the colours are based on a reflection in the water in Venice and the design is a homage to the wonderful Italian designers Missoni. Depending how the handles are sewn on it can also be a backpack. Customise the bag by adding more beads or keepsakes to the cord tie on the bag.

measurements
Length: 38 cm (15 in)
Circumference: 61 cm (24 in)

materials
1 x 50g ball Rowan Pure Wool DK in each of Marine 008 (A), Indigo 010 (B), Hyacinth 026 (C), Hydrangea 027 (D), Cypress 007 (E), Honey 033 (F), Anthracite 003 (G), Port 037 (H), Damson 030 (I), Glade 021 (J) and Hay 014 (K)
Pair 4 mm (US 6) knitting needles
Two 3¾ mm (US 5) double-pointed knitting needles
2 large beads
Darning needle

tension
28 sts (2 pattern repeats) and 28 rows to 11 cm (4¼ in) over patt using 4 mm (US 6) needles.

abbreviations
See page 15.

notes
- Before beginning this project arrange your balls of wool in colour order to make changing colour easier.
- Knit in the ends for a few stitches when changing colour for a neater finish.

main part
Using 4 mm (US 6) needles and H, cast on 156 sts.
K 1 row.
Change to A.
Cont in chevron patt:
1st row: P.
2nd row: K1, [K in front and back of next st, K4, s1, K1, psso, K2tog, K4, K in front and back of next st] to last st, K1.
These 2 rows form patt.
Patt 4 more rows.
* Cont in patt in stripes of 8 rows B, 6 rows each C, D and E, 4 rows F*, 2 rows G, 6 rows each H, I, J, K and A. These 62 rows form stripe sequence.
Rep from * to *.
Change to G.

base shaping
Next row: P.
Next row: K1, [K in front and back of next st, K1, K2tog, K1, s1, K1, psso, K2tog, K1, K2tog, K1, K in front and back of next st] to last st, K1. (134 sts)
Change to H.

Next row: P.
Next row: K1, [K in front and back of next st, K2tog, K1, s1, K1, psso, K2 tog, K1, K2tog, K in front and back of next st] to last st, K1. (112 sts)
Next row: P.
Next row: K1, * K in front and back of next st, K2tog, s1, K1, psso, [K2tog] twice, K in front and back of next st, rep from * to last st, K1. (90 sts)
Next row: P.
Cast off.

handle
Using A, cast on 16 sts.
1st row: P.
2nd row (RS): K1, K in front and back of next st, K4, s1, K1, psso, K2 tog, K4, K in front and back of next st, K1.
Patt 4 rows.
Cont in patt in 62-row stripe sequence of Main Part, until handle measures 66 cm (26 in).
Cast off.

bright & beautiful

cord

Using 4 mm (US 6) double-pointed needles and J, cast on 5 sts.
K 1 row.
Do not turn, slide sts to beg of needle, pulling yarn tightly across back of work, K a second row.
Cont until cord measures 100 cm (39¼ in).
Cast off.

to make up

Press lightly according to instructions on yarn label. Sew base and side seam. Fold handle in half lengthways and slip stitch edges. Sew 2 cm (¾ in) inside side seam and opposite side. For a backpack make a second handle and attach each at top and at base of bag. Thread cord through larger holes at the top of Chevron worked in C. Thread a large bead onto each end and knot to secure. Darn in ends.

Add beads of your choice or keepsakes to the ends of the cord to personalise the bag.

bright & beautiful

fairisle scarf

This warm and cosy scarf is based on a traditional Fairisle pattern, possibly brought to the Islands by shipwrecked Spanish sailors from the Armada. Although the design may look complicated there are never more than 2 colours in a row, and small motifs are repeated with subtle colour changes.

measurements
Width: 15 cm (6 in)
Length (excluding fringe): 158 cm (62 in)

materials
2 x 50 g balls Rowan 4-ply Soft in Dove 394 (A) or Nippy 376 (A)
1 x 50 g ball Rowan 4-ply Soft in each of Folly 391 (B), Linseed 393 (C), Marine 380 (D), Honk 374 (E) and Daydream 378 (F).
Pair 3¼ mm (US 3) knitting needles
Crochet hook
Darning needle

tension
30 sts and 29 rows to 10 cm (4 in) measured over patt using 3¼ mm (US 3) needles.

abbreviations
See page 15.

notes
■ Take care with your tension as knitting Fairisle too tightly will result in a puckered fabric.

scarf
Using A, cast on 90 sts.
Cont in st st from Charts:
** Read odd-numbered (K) rows from right to left and even-numbered (P) rows from left to right.

chart 1
1st row (RS): Rep 12 patt sts to last 6 sts, patt 6 edge sts.
2nd row: Patt 6 edge sts, rep 12 patt sts to end.
Patt 3rd to 44th rows of Chart 1.

chart 2
1st row (RS): Rep 8 patt sts to last 2 sts, patt 2 edge sts.
2nd row: Patt 2 edge sts, rep 8 patt sts to end.
Patt 3rd to 18th rows of Chart 2.

chart 3 (see page 92)
1st row (RS): Rep 24 patt sts to last 18 sts, patt 18 edge sts.
2nd row: Patt 18 edge sts, rep 24 patt sts to end.
Patt 3rd to 31st rows of Chart 3.
As next row is a P row, read odd-numbered (P) rows from left to right and even-numbered (K) rows from right to left and patt 44 rows of Chart 1, 18 rows of Chart 2 and 31 rows of Chart 3. **
Rep from ** to ** until Scarf measures 158 cm (62 in).
Cast off.

to make up
Press according to instructions on yarn label.
With RS facing and using mattress st, join row-ends.

fringe
Wind B six times around a 10 cm (4 in) wide piece of stiff card. Cut along one edge to give six 20 cm (8 in) strands. Fold strands in half. Push crochet hook through both thicknesses of cast-on edge of Scarf and pull folded ends through, then pull cut ends through folded ends and pull tight.
Changing colour each time and spacing fringes evenly, fringe both ends. Press and trim fringe to neaten ends.

bright & beautiful

chart 1

chart 2

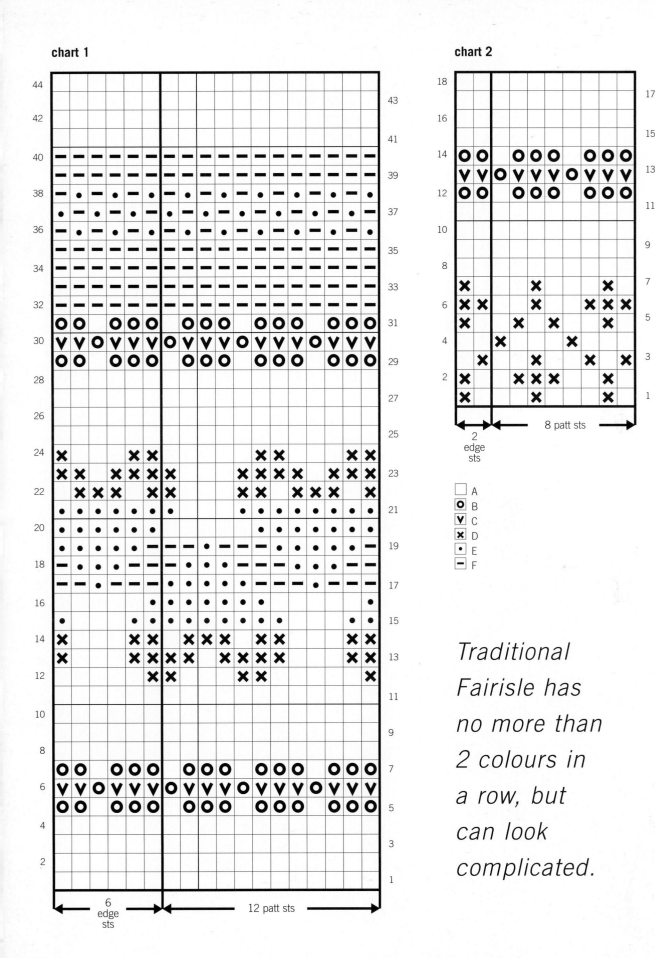

A
B
C
D
E
F

Traditional Fairisle has no more than 2 colours in a row, but can look complicated.

classic
stripes

Cool shades of grey, blue and cream make for a fresh, clean and easy-to-wear striped accessory. Be seen in red and white stripes in the city, and for country walks try tweedy shades of lavender, oatmeal, clover, damson and heather. Toast your toes in claret and chocolate at the end of the day – comforting and comfortable colours.

french beret

Have fun with these berets, use your own colours and place at a jaunty angle. Knit one for each of your outfits or as gifts for friends and family. You could personalise and customise a finished beret by adding badges, ribbons, flowers or bows. The chaps will love one of these as well.

measurement
Circumference at widest point:
58 cm (23 in)

materials
plain beret
1 x 50 g ball Rowan Pure Wool DK in Mocha 017
striped beret
1 x 50 g ball Rowan Pure Wool DK in each of Kiss 036 (A) and Enamel 013 (B)
Pair 3¾ mm (US 5) and 4 mm (US 6) knitting needles
Darning needle

tension
22 sts and 30 rows to 10 cm (4 in) measured over st st using 4 mm (US 6) needles.

abbreviations
See page 15.

note
■ Use the thumb method to cast on as this gives a firm edge.

plain beret
Using 3¾ mm (US 5) needles, cast on 85 sts.
1st row (RS): K1, [P1, K1] to end.
2nd rib row: P1, [K1, P1] to end.
Rep last 2 rows 4 times more.
Change to 4 mm (US 6) needles.
Inc row: [K3, M1] 28 times, K1.
(113 sts)
Beg with a P row, work 11 rows in st st.
Inc row: [K8, M1] 14 times, K1.
(127 sts)
St st 13 rows.

crown shaping
1st row: [K7, K2tog] 14 times, K1.
(113 sts)
St st 5 rows.
7th row: [K13, K3tog] 7 times, K1.
(99 sts)
St st 5 rows.
13th row: [K11, K3tog] 7 times, K1.
(85 sts)
St st 3 rows.
17th row: [K9, K3tog] 7 times, K1.
(71 sts)
St st 3 rows.
21st row: [K7, K3tog] 7 times, K1.

(57 sts)
St st 3 rows.
25th row: [K5, K3tog] 7 times, K1.
(43 sts)
St st 3 rows.
29th row: [K1, K3tog] 7 times, K1.
(29 sts)
P 1 row.
31st row: [K1, K3tog] 7 times, K1.
(15 sts)
Break yarn and thread through rem sts, draw up.

stalk
Using 3¾ mm (US 5) needles, cast on 7 sts.
St st 4 rows.
Cast off.
With RS facing and using mattress stitch, join back seam. Attach stalk to centre top.

striped beret
Work as Plain Beret, casting on with A and working in stripes of 2 rows A and 2 rows B throughout. Use A for Stalk.

To make a
deeper beret
add more rows
before the
crown shaping.

striped socks

Warm and cosy socks to toast your toes, ideal for cold winter days or worn inside wellies in the garden. Work in one colour or many shades of stripes. You could also try adding a small Fairisle motif at the top.

socks

Using 3 mm (US 2) needles and A, cast on 64 sts. Divide sts evenly over 3 needles.

Take a length of contrasting thread and mark beg of round. Carry thread loosley up WS to mark beg of every round – beg of round is centre back.

Work K1, P1 rib for 5 cm (2 in).

Change to 3¼ mm (US 3) needles and B. Cont in st st (every row K) stripe patt of 4 rows B and 4 rows A. (When a colour is changed twist the yarn around the other to prevent a hole.)

Work 28 rounds.

29th round: K1, K2tog, K to last 3 sts, sl 1, K1, psso, K1.

30th round: K.

31st and 32nd rounds: As 29th and 30th rounds. (60 sts)

St st 12 rounds.

45th to 48th rounds: As 29th to 32nd rounds. (56 sts)

St st 16 rounds.

65th to 72nd rounds: Work 29th and 30th rounds 4 times. (48 sts)

Cont straight until work measures 30 cm (12 in) from cast-on edge,

ending with a B stripe. (Adjust length here if required.)

Sl first 12 sts of round onto one needle, sl next 24 sts onto st holder for instep, sl last 12 sts of round onto 2nd needle.

Beg with sts on 2nd needle, work on 24 sts for heel.

heel

Cont in A.

1st row (RS): [Sl1 knitwise, K1] 12 times.

2nd row: Sl1 purlwise, P23.

Rep last 2 rows until heel measures 6.5 cm (2½ in), ending with 2nd row.

heel shaping

1st row: Sl1, K13, sl1, K1, psso, K1, turn.

2nd row: Sl1, P5, P2tog, P1 turn.

3rd row: Sl1, K6, Sl1, K1, psso, K1, turn.

4th row: Sl1, P7, P2tog, P1, turn.

5th row: Sl1, K8, sl1, K1, psso, K1, turn.

6th row: Sl1, P9, P2tog, P1, turn.

7th row: Sl1, K10, sl1, K1, psso, K1, turn.

8th row: Sl1, P11, P2tog, P1, turn.

measurement
To fit a medium foot

materials
2 x 50 g balls Rowan Felted Tweed in Treacle 145 (A)
1 x 50 g ball Rowan Felted Tweed in Rage 150 (B)
Set each of 3 mm (US 2) and 3¼ mm (US 3) double-pointed Knitting needles
St holder
Darning needle

tension
22 sts and 30 rows to 10 cm (4 in) over st st using 3¼ mm (US 3) needles.

abbreviations
See page 15.

note
■ Add nylon thread to the heel for extra strength.

Note the reinforced heel – when the colour is changed twist one yarn around the other to prevent a hole forming.

9th row: Sl1, K12, sl1, K1, psso, turn.

10th row: Sl1, P12, P2tog, turn. (14 sts)

Next row (RS): K14, pick up and K14 sts along row-ends of 1st side of heel, K24 instep sts from st holder, pick up and K14 sts along row-ends of 2nd side of heel. (66 sts) Starting at centre back s1 21 sts onto 1st needle, 24 sts of instep onto 2nd needle and rem 21 sts onto 3rd needle.

Work next 3 rounds in A, then beg with B, cont in st st stripes.

1st round: K.

2nd round: K to last 3 sts on 1st needle, K2tog, K1; K across 24 sts on 2nd needle; across sts on 3rd needle work K1, sl1, K1, psso, K to end.

Rep last 2 rounds 8 times. (48 sts)

Work 29 rounds straight, ending with a complete stripe in B. (Adjust length here if required.)

Cont in A.

toe shaping

1st round: K to last 3 sts on 1st needle, K2tog, K1; across sts on 2nd needle work K1, sl1, K1, psso, K to last 3 sts, K2tog, K1; across sts on 3rd needle work K1, sl1, K1, psso, K to end. (44 sts)

2nd round: K.

Rep last 2 rounds until 20 sts rem. Sl 5 sts from 3rd needle onto 1st needle.

With right sides tog cast off taking one st from each needle tog each time.

to make up

Press according to instructions on yarn label.

Darn in ends.

classic stripes

jazzy stripes hat

This classic hat is worked in crunchy-textured garter stitch throughout. Stripes in any combination are always in vogue. Why not choose your own colours – soft pastel shades, browns and greens or blues and pinks – or keep it simple by sticking to one colour.

measurement
Circumference: 52 cm (20½ in)

materials
1 x 50 g ball Rowan Pure Wool DK in each of Glacier 005 (A), Enamel 013 (B) and Marine 008 (C)
Pair 4 mm (US 6) knitting needles
Darning needle

tension
21 sts and 40 rows to 10 cm (4 in) measured over gst using 4 mm (US 6) needles.

abbreviations
See page 15.

note
■ Sew yarn ends down the side seams to keep them invisible.

hat

Using C, cast on 110 sts.
Joining in at beg and fastening off at end of each stripe, cont in gst.
Work in stripes of 8 rows each C, A and B.
These 24 rows form stripe patt.
Cont until a total of 47 rows have been completed, ending with 7th row of 2nd B stripe.

shape crown

Keep striped sequence correct.

1st row: K1, [K3tog, K12] 7 times, K4. (96 sts)
K 4 rows.
6th row: K1, [K3tog, K10] 7 times, K4. (82 sts)
K 4 rows.
11th row: K1, [K3tog, K8] 7 times, K4. (68 sts)
K4 rows.
16th row: K1, [K3tog, K6] 7 times, K4. (54 sts)
K4 rows.
21st row: K1, [K3tog, K4] 7 times, K4. (40 sts)
K4 rows.
26th row: K1, [K3tog, K2] 7 times, K4. (26 sts)
K 4 rows.
31st row: K1, [K2tog] to last st, K1. (14 sts)
K 1 row.
33rd row: [K2tog] to end. (7 sts)
Break yarn and thread through rem sts, draw up.
Join back seam.

to make up

Make a pom-pom (see page 46) using yarns A, B and C. Sew pom-pom to top of hat.

44

jazzy stripes scarf

Wear this fun scarf alone or combine it with the Jazzy Stripes Hat on pages 44–45; either way it's sure to become a firm favourite. For a different look you could replace the pop-poms with beads or keepsakes, or a design of your own. Get creative and let your imagination take over!

measurements

Width: 29 cm (11½ in)
Length: 127 cm (50 in)

materials

2 x 50 g balls Rowan Pure Wool DK in each of Glacier 005 (A), Enamel 013 (B) and Marine 008 (C)
Pair of 4 mm (US 6) knitting needles
Darning needle

tension

21 sts and 40 rows to 10 cm (4 in) measured over gst using 4 mm (US 6) needles.

abbreviations

See page 15.

scarf

Using A, cast on 60 sts.
Joining in at beg and fastening off at end of each stripe, cont in gst.
Work in stripes of 8 rows each A, B and C.
These 24 rows form stripe patt.
Cont in stripe patt until the scarf measures 127 cm (50 in), ending with a completed stripe.
Cast off.

to make a pom-pom

Cut two circles 5 cm (2 in) in diameter from stiff card. Cut out a 2.5 cm (1 in) circle in the centre of each larger circle. Place the two larger circles together and using 1 m (1 yd) lengths of yarn wind the yarn around the two circles and through the centre hole. Cont until hole is full. (You may need to use a darning needle threaded with the yarn to fill the centre completely.) Push the point of a pair of scissors between the two circles of card and cut around the strands of yarn. Place a length of yarn between the two circles of card and tie tightly, leaving a long end to sew the pom-pom on the scarf (or hat). Tear the card away from the pom-pom and trim ends of yarn to give a neat rounded shape.

to make up

Darn in ends.
Make 3 pom-poms in A, 2 in B and 3 in C. Sew 4 pom-poms to each end of scarf mixing the colours, as shown in the photograph.

classic stripes

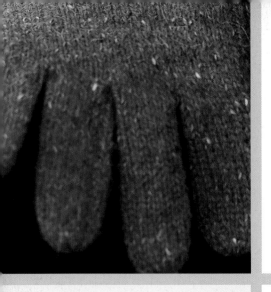

striped gloves

Suitable for men or women, just change the colour to suit. Knit in one colour, stripe throughout or leave the fingers half knitted and cast off for fingerless gloves. This is a really versatile pattern – presents for all the family, sorted!

measurement
Circumference around palm: 21 cm (8¼ in)

materials
1 x 50g ball Rowan Felted Tweed in each of Midnight 133 (A) and Bilberry 151 (B)
Pair each 2¾ mm (US 2) and 3 mm (US 3) knitting needles
Darning needle
Few metres (yards) of a similar yarn in a colour to contrast with gloves

tension
28 sts and 36 rows to 10 cm (4 in) measured over st st using 3 mm (US 3) needles.

abbreviations
See page 15.

note
■ Use a bright contrast coloured yarn (e.g. yellow) for the thumb shaping. The stitches to be picked up will be more visible.

left glove
Using 2¾ mm (US 2) needles and A, cast on 58 sts.
1st row (RS): K.
2nd row: P.
Work 10 cm (4 in) K1, P1 rib, ending with a RS row.
Change to 3 mm (US 3) needles.
Beg with a P row, st st 5 rows.
St st 10 rows B.
St st 5 rows A, ending with a K row, do not fasten.

thumb opening
With WS facing and using contrast coloured yarn, K 10 sts, turn and K back. Work 6 more rows on these 10 sts with this yarn and break off contrast. This completes thumb opening (the contrast yarn will be unpicked when thumb is worked).
Next row: With WS facing and A, P across the 10 sts in contrast yarn, P rem 48 sts. (58 sts)
St st 4 rows.
Change to B and st st 10 rows.
Change to A and st st 2 rows.

divide for fingers
Fingers are worked in A.
little finger
1st row (RS): K36, turn.
2nd row: P14, turn.
St st 18 rows on these 14 sts.
Dec row: K2, [K2tog, K1] 4 times. (10 sts)
* Work 2 rows, break yarn and thread through sts, draw up and fasten off securely. Join seam.*

third finger
1st row (RS): With RS facing, pick up and K2 sts from base of Litte Finger, K7, turn.
2nd row: P16, turn.
St st 24 rows on these 16 sts.
Dec row: [K1, K2tog, K1] 4 times. (12 sts)
Work as little finger from * to *.

middle finger
Work as Third Finger, picking up sts from base of Third Finger and working 2 extra rows before Dec row.

first finger
1st row (RS): With RS facing, pick up and K2 sts from base of Middle Finger, K8, turn.
2nd row: P18.
St st 22 rows.
Dec row: [K2, K2tog, K1] 4 times, K1. (17 sts)

classic stripes

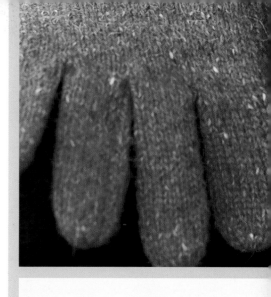

Work as Litte Finger from * to *.

thumb

With WS facing and A and working into sts of last row in A before the 1st row in contrast yarn, P10, pick up and P strand between sts, P into the base of each of 10 sts of first row in A at top of Thumb opening. (21 sts) Cut and carefully unravel the contrast yarn.

St st 24 rows.

Dec row: [K2, K2tog, K1] 4 times, K1. (17 sts)

Work as Little Finger from * to *.

to make up

Join seam closing any gaps at the base of the fingers.

right glove

Work as Left Glove but place the thumb on the reverse side and reverse all shapings to match.

These gloves are so easy to knit you could make a pair to match every outfit.

cloche hat

An alchemy of colours conjures up heather hillsides and bramble hedges in this cosy hat. This really easy pattern can be completed in a weekend. Work in one colour only or alternate stripes. Note the tiny turn back brim in reverse stocking stitch which gives the hat a stylish finish.

measurement
Actual measurement: 56 cm
(22 in)

materials
1 x 25g ball Rowan Scottish Tweed
4 ply in each of Winter Navy 021
(A), Celtic Mix 022 (B), Mallard
020 (C), Blue Mist 027 (D) and
Sea Green 006 (E).
Pair 2¾ mm (US 2) and 3 mm (US
3) knitting needles.
Darning needle

tension
23 sts and 40 rows to 10 cm (4 in)
measured over st st using 3 mm
(US 3) needles.

abbreviations
See page 15.

note
■ For a deeper hat knit extra rows
before the crown shaping.

hat

Using 2¾ mm (US 2) needles and A,
cast on 128 sts.
1st row (RS): P.
2nd row: K.
Rep these 2 rows 3 times more.
Change to 3 mm (US 3) needles.
Joining in at beg and fastening off at
end of each stripe, and beg with a K
row, cont in st st in stripes of 4 rows
each B, C, D, E and A.
These 20 rows form stripe patt.
Work 20 more rows.

shape crown

1st row: K1, [K3tog, K18] 6 times,
K1. (116 sts)
Patt 3 rows.
5th row: K1, [K3tog, K16] 6 times,
K1. (104 sts)
Patt 3 rows.
9th row: K1, [K3tog, K14] 6 times,
K1. (92 sts)
Patt 3 rows.
13th row: K1, [K3tog, K12] 6 times,
K1. (80 sts)
Patt 3 rows.
17th row: K1, [K3tog, K10] 6 times,
K1. (68 sts)
Patt 3 rows.

21st row: K1, [K3tog, K8] 6 times,
K1. (56 sts)
Patt 3 rows.
25th row: K1, [K3tog, K6] 6 times,
K1. (44 sts)
Patt 3 rows.
29th row: K1, [K3tog, K4] 6 times,
K1. (32 sts)
Patt 3 rows.
33rd row: K1, [K3tog, K2] 6 times,
K1. (20 sts)
Patt 3 rows.
37th row: K1, [K2tog] to last st, K1.
(10 sts)
Patt 1 row.
Break off yarn, thread end through
rem 10 sts, draw up.

to make up

Press lightly, avoiding the bottom
edge. Join centre back seam.
Darn in ends.

classic stripes

neutral shades

Celtic carvings in granite and sandstone within a misty
landscape are the inspiration for shades of antique cream,
pearl, oatmeal, grey mist, moonstone and linen.
Truly classic, calming and restful shades with a
contemporary feel.

cable bag

A variety of very easy chunky cables combined with a touch of moss stitch make this fluffy, soft bag. Steeped in history, cables of various sizes were found in fisherman's sweaters and make a dramatic encrusted, textured fabric which provide inspiration for this bag.

measurements

Depth: 29 cm (11½ in)
Width: 28 cm (11 in)

materials

7 x 50g balls Rowan Little Big Wool in Quartz 506
Pair each 8 mm (US 11) and 7½ mm (US 10½) knitting needles
Two double-pointed 8 mm (US 11) knitting needles
Cable needle
Darning needle
Large button

tension

12 sts and 19 rows to 10 cm (4 in) over st st using 8 mm (US 11) needles.

abbreviations

See page 15.

note

■ This cable design looks difficult to master but really isn't once you get the hang of it.

back

With 8 mm (US 11) needles, cast on 40 sts.
Work in moss st.
1st row: [K1, P1] to end.
2nd row (RS): [P1, K1] to end.
Rep last 2 rows 3 times.
Cast on 10 sts at beg of next 2 rows. (60 sts)
Cont in cable patt:
1st row: [K2, P6, K2] 6 times.
2nd row (RS): [P2, K6, P2] 6 times.
3rd row: [K2, P6, K2] 6 times.
4th row: [P2, C6B – sl next 3 sts onto cable needle and hold at back, K3 then K3 from cable needle, P2] 6 times.
5th to 8th rows: Rep 1st and 2nd rows twice.
These 8 rows form patt.
Cont in patt until work measures 33 cm (13 in).
Work 3 rows moss st.
Cast off.
Work Front to match.

flap

With 8 mm (US 11) needles, cast on 40 sts.
1st row: [K2, P4, K2] 5 times.

2nd row (RS): Inc in first st, P1, K4, P2, [P2, K4, P2] 4 times.
3rd row: Inc in first st, K1, P4, K2, [K2, P4, K2] 4 times, K1.
4th row: Inc in first st, [P2, C4B – sl next 2 sts onto cable needle and hold at back, K2 then K2 from cable needle, P2] 5 times, P1.
5th row: Inc in first st, [K2, P4, K2] 5 times, K2.
6th row: Inc in first st, P1, [P2, K4, P2] 5 times, P2.
7th row: Inc in first st, K1, [K2, P4, K2] 5 times, K2, P1.
8th row: Inc in first st, P2, [P2, C4B, P2] 5 times. P2, K1.
9th row: Inc in first st, K2, [K2, P4, K2] 5 times, K2, P2. (48 sts)
Mark each of last row with a coloured thread.
10th row: K2, P2, [P2, K4, P2] 5 times, P2, K2.
11th row: P2, K2, [K2, P4, K2] 5 times, K2, P2.
With sts as set, and twisting cables on next and every foll 4th row, cont in patt until flap measures 25 cm (10 in).
Cast off.

neutral shades

neutral shades

flap edging

Using double-pointed 8 mm (US 11) needles, cast on 5 sts.

1st row (RS): K5, do not turn, slide sts to beg of needle, pull yarn tightly across back of work.

Rep 1st row 3 times.

5th row: K1, sl next st onto cable needle, hold at front, K2 then K st from cable needle, K1, do not turn, slide sts to beg of needle, pull yarn tightly across back of work.

Rep 1st to 5th rows until work measures 51 cm (20 in).

Cast off.

handle

Using 7½ mm (US 10½) needles, cast on 13 sts.

1st row (RS): P2, K9, P2.

2nd row: K2, P9, K2.

3rd row: P2, sl next 3 sts on to cable needle and hold at front, K3, then K3 from cable needle, K3, P2.

4th row: K2, P9, K2.

5th row: P2, K9, P2.

6th row: K2, P9, K2.

7th row: P2, K3, sl next 3 sts on to cable needle and hold at back, K3 then K3 from cable needle, P2.

8th row: K2, P9, K2.

These 8 rows form patt.

Cont in patt until Handle measures 68 cm (27 in).

Cast off.

to make up

Press lightly according to instructions on yarn label.

Join cast-on edges of Back and Front. Join side seams sewing cast-on groups to row-ends of moss st.

Beg and ending 6 cm (2¼ in) from side seams, sew cast-off edge of Flap to top of Back.

Beg and ending at markers and twisting centre to form a loop for button, sew Flap Edging to lower edge of flap.

Centring ends over side seams, sew on Handle.

Sew button to Front

Cut a piece of stiff card 33 cm (13 in) x 11 cm (4¼ in). Cover with a piece of fabric and glue in place.

Place in base of bag to give shape.

This button complements the cable design perfectly.

celtic wrap

Although this looks complicated, all the individual cables and patterns are very easy and well worth the effort. The centre panel of wave cables represents the shifting sands and waves on an isolated shore and are surrounded by bobbles and crunchy cables in a wonderful soft marled yarn. Wear it or throw it over your comfortable chair.

measurements
Width: 64 cm (25 in)
Length (excluding fringe): 173 cm (68 in)

materials
16 x 50g balls Rowan Scottish Tweed DK in Porridge 042
Pair 4 mm (US 6) knitting needles
Cable needle
Crochet hook
Darning needle

abbreviations
See page 15.

tension
22 sts and 28 rows to 10 cm (4 in) measured over st st using 4 mm (US 6) needles.

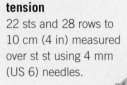

wrap
Cast on 168 sts.
1st row (WS): Reading each chart from left to right, patt row 1 of charts A, B, C, D, E, F, E, D, C, B and A.
2nd row: Reading each chart from right to left, patt row 2 of charts A, B, C, D, E, F, E, D, C, B and A.
Beg with row 3 of each chart, cont in this way reading WS rows from left to right and RS rows from right to left,

until a total of 528 rows have been completed.
Cast off.

to make up
Darn in ends. Wind yarn around a 10 cm (4 in) wide piece of stiff card. Cut along one edge to give 20 cm (8 in) lengths. Take 3 lengths tog and fold in half. Push crochet hook through cast-on edge from WS to RS and pull folded ends of yarn through, pull cut ends through folded ends and pull tight. Fringe both ends in this way, working into every 3rd or 4th st. Press and trim fringe to neaten ends. Press wrap according to instructions on yarn label.

chart A

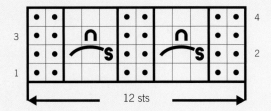

chart B

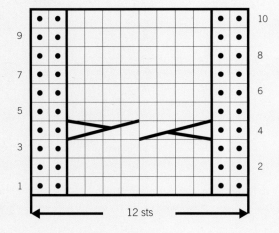

chart C

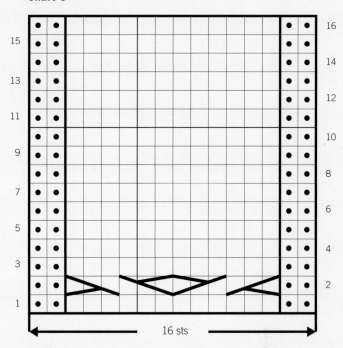

chart D

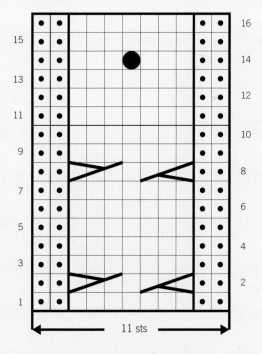

☐ K on RS rows; P on WS rows

• P on RS rows; K on WS rows

∩ yrn

● Make Bobble - (K1,yf, K1 yf, K1) in same st, turn; K5, turn; P5, turn; sl1, K1, psso, K1, K2tog, turn; P3 tog

Sl 1, K2, pass slipped st over the 2K sts

Sl 3 sts onto cable needle, hold at back of work, K4 then K3 from cable needle

Sl 4 sts onto cable needle, hold at back of work, K4 then K4 from cable needle

Sl 3 sts onto cable needle, hold at back of work, K3 then K3 from cable needle; sl 3 sts onto cable needle, hold at front of work, K3 then K3 from cable needle

chart E

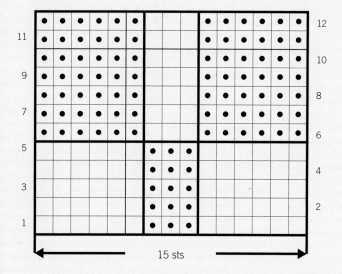

15 sts

chart F

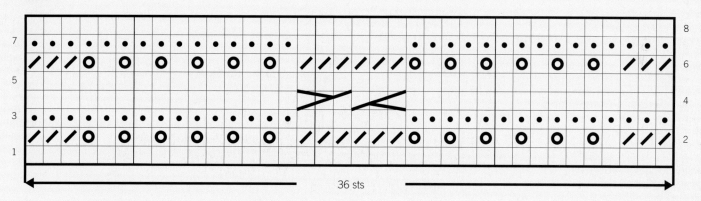

36 sts

☐ K on RS rows; P on WS rows

• P on RS rows; K on WS rows

◪ K2tog

◉ yf

SI 3 sts onto cable needle, hold at
back of work, K3 the K3 from
cable needle

neutral shades   65

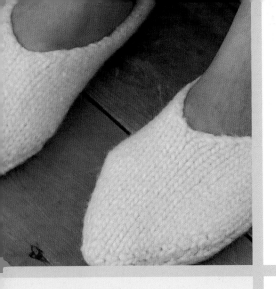

felted slippers

Knit a pair of slippers for your whole family to keep their toes toasty. Add your own embellishments – flowers, knitted bows, pom poms – or embroider on the felted surface. Ideal for taking away on holiday as they take up no room at all.

measurements

Approx length: 22 cm (8¾ in)
Width across sole: 10 cm (4 in) after felting

materials

2 x 50g balls Rowan Little Big Wool in Quartz 506
Pair of 7 mm (US 10½) knitting needles
Darning needle

tension (before felting)

13 sts and 20 rows to 10 cm (4 in) measured over st st using 7 mm (US 10½) needles.

abbreviations

See page 15.

notes

- Use your tension square to test the felting before you try with your slippers.
- Always felt the slippers together.

sole

Cast on 4 sts.
Work in st st throughout.
K 1 row.

toe shaping

Inc 1 st at beg of every row until there are 16 sts.
St st 9 rows straight.
Dec 1 st at beg of next 2 rows.
(14 sts)
Cont straight until work measures 22 cm (8¾ in) from beg, (add extra rows here for a longer slipper).

heel shaping

Dec 1 st at each end of every row until 4 sts rem.

Work 1 row.
Cast off.

upper

Cast on 4 sts.
K 1 row.
Inc 1 st at beg of every row until there are 20 sts.
St st 5 rows straight.
Next row: K 10 sts, turn. Cont on these sts only for 1st side.
* Dec 1 st at beg of every P row until 5 sts rem.
Cont straight until work measures 9 cm (3½ in) from last dec.
Cast off.
With RS facing, rejoin yarn to inner end of rem 10 sts, K to end.
Complete to match 1st side from * but dec at end of P rows.

to make up

Join cast-off edges of upper.
Pin the upper to the sole and stitch in place.
Place in the washing machine with a towel and wash at 60°. Stretch and mould into shape. Allow to dry naturally.

cobweb shawl

Oh so fine and soft, this shawl is ideal for summer weddings and adds a feminine touch to denim and leather. The addition of tiny beads around the edge adds extra interest – try changing the colour to suit your mood or leave the beads off completely for a more casual look.

measurements
Top edge: 150 cm (59 in)
Depth to point: 46 cm (18 in)

materials
1 x 25 g ball Rowan Kidsilk Haze in Cream 634
Pair of 5 mm (US 8) knitting needles
Approx 200 small white pearl beads
Beading needle
Darning needle

tension
10 sts and 12 rows to 10 cm (4 in) over patt using 5 mm (US 8) needles.

abbreviations
See page 15.

shawl

Cast on 3 sts.

K 4 rows.

5th row: K into front and back of first st, [K1, yf] to last st, K1.

6th row: K to end dropping each yf. (4 sts)

Rep 5th and 6th rows until there are 46 sts, ending with a 6th row.

Next row: K2tog, [K1, yf] to last st, K1.

Next row: As 6th row. (45 sts)

Rep last 2 rows until 3 sts rem, ending with a 6th row.

K 4 rows.

Cast off.

Darn in ends.

Thread the beading needle with a length of yarn and sew a bead at the end of each row on both short sides.

neutral shades

fingerless gloves

These fingerless gloves are knitted in the same luxurious yarn as the Cobweb Shawl on pages 68–69. The two designs look gorgeous together or can be worn apart as a practical fashion statement. Team them with pastel shades on a warm summer's day or with strong colours to keep hands cosy in winter.

measurements

To fit average lady's hand
Length: 39 cm (15¼ in)

materials

1 x 25g ball Rowan Kidsilk Haze in Cream 634
Pair of 3¾ mm (US 5) knitting needles
2 stitch holders
Darning needle

tension

22 sts and 31 rows to 10 cm (4 in) over rib using 3¾ mm (US 8) needles.

abbreviations

See page 15.

right glove

Cast on 46 sts.

1st row: P.

2nd row (RS): K.

Rep the last 2 rows once more.

Work in K1, P1 rib for 30 cm (11¾ in), ending with a WS row. *

thumb shaping

1st row (RS): Rib 28, [inc in next st] twice, rib 16. (48 sts)

2nd row: Rib 16, P4, rib 28.

3rd row: Rib 28, inc in next st, K2, inc in next st, rib 16. (50 sts)

4th row: Rib 16, P6, rib 28.

5th row: Rib 28, inc in next st, K 4, inc in next st, rib 16. (52 sts)

Working 2 more sts between incs each time, cont to inc in this way on next 3 RS rows. (58 sts)

Next row: Rib 16, P14, rib 28.

divide for thumb

1st row (RS): Rib 28, inc in next st, K 12, inc in next st, turn. Leave rem 16 sts on a st holder.

2nd row: P15, turn. Leave rem 29 sts on a st holder.

3rd row: K15.

4th row: P15.

Cast off. Join thumb seam.

Next row: With RS facing, pick up and K 1 st from base of thumb, rib 16 sts from st holder.

** **Next row:** Rib across all 46 sts.

Rib 12 rows.

K 1 row.

P 1 row.

Cast off.

Join side seam.

left glove

Work as right glove to *.

thumb shaping

1st row (RS): Rib 15, [inc in next st] twice, rib 29. (48 sts)

2nd row: Rib 29, P4, rib 15.

neutral shades

3rd row: Rib 15, inc in next st, K2, inc in next st, rib 29. (50 sts)

4th row: Rib 29, P6, rib 15.

5th row: Rib 15, inc in next st, K4, inc in next st, rib 29. (52 sts)

Working 2 more sts between incs each time, cont to inc in this way on next 3 RS rows. (58 sts)

Next row: Rib 29, P14, rib 15.

divide for thumb

1st row (RS): Rib 15, inc in next st, K 12, inc in next st, turn. Leave rem 29 sts on a st holder.

2nd row: P15, turn. Leave rem 16 sts on a st holder.

3rd row: K15.

4th row: P15.

Cast off.

Join thumb seam.

Next row: With RS facing pick up and K 1 st from base of thumb, rib 29 sts from st holder.

Complete as Right Glove from **.

This soft, fluffy yarn looks great and will keep you snug on cold days.

neutral shades

string bag

You will be amazed how much this bag will carry and with its stylish shape you'll want to take it everywhere you go. Worked in a very simple stitch to emulate the shopping bag your mother used to make in natural linen coloured cotton. It also looks good in denim cotton.

measurements

Depth: Approx. 32 cm (12½ in)
Width: Approx. 34 cm (13¼ in)

materials

5 x 50 g balls Rowan Handknit
Cotton in Linen 205
Pair of 4 mm (US 6) knitting
needles
Two 4 mm (US 6) double-pointed
needles
30 cm (12 in) of 2 cm (¾ in) wide
elastic
Darning needle

tension

20 sts and 28 rows to 10 cm (4 in)
measured over patt using 4 mm
(US 6) needles.

abbreviations

See page 15.

notes

- Although a very easy stitch it is
  very difficult to unpick a row if a
  mistake is made so take extra
  care.
- Make the handle longer for a
  shoulder bag.

bag

Using pair of 4 mm (US 6) needles,
cast on 30 sts.
1st row: P.
2nd row: K into front and back of
each st. (60 sts)
Cont in patt:
1st row: K1, [take yarn from back
over and around right needle to
make a stitch, K2tog] to last st, K1.
2nd row (RS): K2, [K into front (left
strand) of made st, K1] to end.
These 2 rows form patt.
Cont in patt inc 1 st at each end of
every RS row until there are 68 sts.
Patt straight until work measures
27 cm (10½ in), ending with a RS
row.
Next row: P.
Next row: K1, [K2tog] to last st, K1.
(35 sts)
Beg with a P row, work 8 cm (3 in)
in st st.
Cast off loosely.
Make another piece to match.

to make up

Fold st st sections at top in half to
WS. Leaving ends open, sew cast-off
edge in place. With right sides facing
and beg 12 cm (4¾ in) from fold at
top, join side and base seams.

side handle carrier

Using pair of 4 mm (US 6) needles,
with RS facing, and beg at top fold,
pick up and K 18 sts down first side
to side seam, taking care to pick up
sts on outside piece only of folded
top, then pick up and K 18 sts up
other side. (36 sts).
Beg with a P row, work 10 rows st st.
Cast off.
Fold in half to WS and leaving ends
open, sew cast-off edge in place.
Work other side to match.

neutral shades

handle

Using 4 mm (US 6) double-pointed needles and yarn double, cast on 4 sts.

K1 row.

Do not turn, slide sts to beg of needle, pulling yarn tightly across back of work, K a second row. Cont until handle measures 140 cm (55 in).

Cast off.

Thread through one handle carrier then through 2nd. Sew ends of handle firmly and slide around until the join is hidden.

Draw up the handles of the bag. Cut elastic in half. Thread through folded top of Front and Back. Sew firmly into place. On WS sew open ends to handle carriers.

Press lightly.

Thread the cord down one handle carrier and up and down the next to join the ends before sewing together.

neutral shades

cable socks

Soft and creamy, these luxurious socks worked in delicate cables to a traditional Aran diamond pattern are ideal for slouchy days and are set to become a favourite for cold evenings. Make a longer leg version to wear inside winter boots and wellies.

measurement
To fit medium foot

materials
4 x 50 g balls Rowan Cashsoft DK in Cream 500
Pair each of 2¾ mm (US 2) and 3 mm (US 3) knitting needles
One 3 mm (US 3) double-pointed needle
Cable needle
2 stitch holders
Darning needle

tension
26 sts and 35 rows to 10 cm (4 in) measured over st st using 3 mm (US 3) needles.

abbreviations
See page 15.

notes
■ Use yellow sticky notes to flag the row you are working on.
■ These are soft socks and will not be very hard wearing but if you choose a yarn with a nylon content they will last much longer.

stitch patterns
The cable socks are worked in two textured stitch patterns, Mock Cable and Aran Diamond.

mock cable
(worked over 26 sts)
1st row: [K2, P2] 6 times, K2.
2nd row (RS): [P2, K2] 6 times, P2.
3rd row: As 1st row.
4th row: [P2, K into front of 2nd st on left needle then K into back of first st and sl both sts off left needle tog] 6 times, P2.
These 4 rows form Mock Cable patt.

aran diamond
(worked over 15 sts)
1st row: K6, P1, K1, P1, K6.
2nd row (RS): P6, sl next 2 sts onto cable needle and hold at front, K1 tbl, sl P st from cable needle back onto left needle and P1, K1 tbl from cable needle, P6.
3rd row: As 1st row.
4th row: P5, C2R – sl next st onto cable needle and hold at back, K1 tbl then P st from cable needle, K1, C2L – sl next st onto cable needle and hold at front, P1 then K tbl st from cable needle, P5.

5th and all WS rows: K the K sts and P the P sts.
6th row: P4, C2R, K1, P1, K1, C2L, P4.
8th row: P3, C2R, [K1, P1] twice, K1, C2L, P3.
10th row: P2, C2R, [K1, P1] 3 times, K1, C2L, P2.
12th row: P1, C2R, [K1, P1] 4 times, K1, C2L, P1.
14th row: P1, C2L, [P1, K1] 4 times, P1, C2R, P1.
16th row: P2, C2L, [P1, K1] 3 times, P1, C2R, P2.
18th row: P3, C2L, [P1, K1] twice, P1, C2R, P3.
20th row: P4, C2L, P1, K1, P1, C2R, P4.
22nd row: P5, C2L, P1, C2R, P5.
These 22 rows form Aran Diamond.

socks
Using 2¾ mm (US 2) needles, cast on 67 sts.
1st rib row: K1 tbl, [P1, K1 tbl] to end.
2nd rib row (RS): P1, [K1 tbl, P1] to end.
Rep these 2 rows 3 times more.

Change to 3 mm (US 3) needles.
Cont in patt:

1st row: Patt 26 sts of 1st row of
Mock Cable patt, patt 15 sts of 1st
row of Aran Diamond, patt 26 sts of
1st row of Mock Cable patt.

With sts as set, patt 66 more rows,
ending with 1st row of 4th diamond.
Fasten off. (If you want longer socks
add more rows here.)

divide for instep

1st row (RS): Sl first 19 sts onto a st

holder, patt 29 sts, turn and leave
rem 19 sts on a st holder.
With sts as set, cont in patt on
centre 29 sts.
Patt 45 rows, ending with 3rd row of
6th diamond

neutral shades

Length of foot can be adjusted here.
Fasten off.

Leave these sts on a spare needle.

heel

With RS facing sl sts from st holders onto one needle with back leg seam at centre. (38 sts)

Patt 20 rows as set for back of heel.

heel shaping

1st row (RS): K28, sl 1, K1, psso, turn.

2nd row: P19, P2tog, turn.

3rd row: K19, sl 1, K1, psso, turn.

4th row: As 2nd row.

Rep 3rd and 4th rows until 20 sts rem, ending with a P row.

Fasten off.

Next row (RS): Pick up and K16 sts along 1st side of back of heel, K20 sts of back of heel, pick up and K16 sts along 2nd side of back of heel. (52 sts)

Next row: P.

side shaping

Next row: K1, sl 1, K1, psso, K to last 3 sts, K2tog, K1.

Next row: K1, P to last st, K1.

Rep these 2 rows until 40 sts rem.

Cont straight until side edges measure 3 cm (1¼ in) less than upper, ending with a P row.

Next row: K1, sl 1, K1, psso, K to last 3 sts, K2tog, K1.

Next row: P.

Rep these 2 rows 4 times. (30 sts)

toe

1st row (RS): Across sts of sole [K1 tb1l, P1] 6 times, K1 tbl, P2tog, [K1 tbl, P1] 7 times, K1 tbl; across sts of upper, [K1 tbl, P1] 14 times, K1 tbl. (58 sts)

2nd row: [P1, K1 tbl] 14 times, P1, [P1, K1 tbl] 14 times, P1.

1st dec row: [Sl 1, K1, psso, rib 25, K2tog] twice. (54 sts)

Rib 1 row.

2nd dec row: [Sl 1, K1, psso, rib 23, K2tog] twice. (50 sts)

Rib 1 row.

3rd dec row: [Sl 1, K1, psso, rib 21, K2tog] twice. (46 sts)

Rib 1 row.

4th dec row: [Sl 1, K1, psso, rib 19, K2tog] twice. (42 sts)

Rib 1 row.

5th dec row: [Sl 1, K1, psso, rib 17, K2tog] twice. (38 sts)

Rib 1 row.

join toe seam

Sl first 19 sts onto double pointed needle and with RS tog cast off taking one st from each needle tog each time.

to make up

Press according to instructions on yarn label.

Join centre back and foot seams.

Darn in ends.

Neatly graft the toe seam together by using a third needle – insert into the first stitch on each needle and knit as one stitch.

feather & fan scarf

A smaller version of the Feather & Fan Wrap on pages 26–27, this pretty scarf will complement any outfit. Why not try experimenting with different coloured yarns to suit your mood, or add stripes in bright colours for a fun and funky look. The feather and fan pattern is so lovely you'll want to knit this design time and time again.

measurements
Width: 40 cm (15¾ in)
Length: 137 cm (54 in)

materials
4 x 50 g balls Rowan Kid Classic in Feather 828
Pair 5 mm (US 8) knitting needles
Darning needle

tension
18 sts and 20 rows to 8 cm (3⅛ in) measured over Feather and Fan patt using 5 mm (US 8) needles.

abbreviations
See page 15.

note
■ Wrap light-coloured yarns, such as the one used for this scarf, in a clean towel when not in use to stop them getting dirty.

feather and fan patt
(multiple of 18 sts)
1st row (RS): K.
2nd row: P.
3rd row: * (K2tog) 3 times, (yo, K1) 6 times, (K2tog) 3 times, rep from * to end.
4th row: P.
These 4 rows form Feather and Fan patt.

scarf
Using 5 mm (US 8) needles cast on 90 sts. Work in Feather and Fan patt until Scarf measures 138 cm (54 in), ending with a 4th patt row.
Cast off.

to make up
Darn in ends. Press according to instructions on yarn label.

neutral shades

fun & funky

Fun to knit and wear. Timeless classics worked in funky colours and updated Fairisle, full of zing and spirit. Rambling roses winding their way around your shoulders, so feminine yet not insipid. Team with plaited denim fingerless gloves –
anything goes.

fairisle legwarmers

Warm and lovely, these Fairisle legwarmers are worked in contemporary colours which enhances the design. Change to a dark background yarn for a very different look, or choose your own colours to express yourself and complement your wardrobe.

measurements

Length: 43 cm (17 in)
Circumference: 24 cm (9½ in)

materials

2 x 50 g balls Rowan Pure Wool DK in Clay 001 (A)
1 x 50 g ball Rowan Pure Wool DK in each of Parsley 020 (B), Hay 014 (C), Marine 008 (D), Kiss 036 (E), Hydrangea 027 (F) and Glade 021 (G).
Pair of 3¼ mm (US 3) and 4 mm (US 6) knitting needles
Darning needle

tension

27 sts and 30 rows to 10 cm (4 in) over patt using 4 mm (US 6) needles.

abbreviations

See page 15.

note

- Use yellow sticky notes on the chart to let you know which row you are working.

legwarmers

Using 3¼ mm (US 3) needles and A, cast on 66 sts.
1st row (RS): P2, [K2, P2] to end.
2nd row: K2, [P2, K2] to end.
Rep these 2 rows until work measures 12 cm (4¾ in), ending with a 1st row.
P1 row.
** Change to 4 mm (US 6) needles.
Cont in st st from Charts:
Read odd-numbered (K) rows from right to left and even-numbered (P) rows from left to right.

chart 1 (see page 89)

1st row (RS): Rep 12 patt sts to last 6 sts, patt 6 edge sts.
2nd row: Patt 6 edge sts, rep 12 patt sts to end.
Patt 3rd to 36th rows of Chart 1.

chart 2 (see page 89)

1st row (RS): Rep 8 patt sts to last 2 sts, patt 2 edge sts.
2nd row: Patt 2 edge sts, rep 8 patt sts to end.
Patt 3rd to 14th rows of Chart 2.

chart 3 (see page 92)

1st row (RS): Rep 24 patt sts to last 18 sts, patt 18 edge sts.
2nd row: Patt 18 edge sts, rep 24 patt sts to end.
Patt 3rd to 31st rows of Chart 3.
Patt 1st to 7th rows of Chart 1.
Cont in A.
Change to 3¼ mm (US 3) needles.
Next row: [K1, P1] to end.
Rep last row once.
Cast off loosely.

to make up

Press according to instructions on yarn label.
With RS facing and using mattress st, join centre back seams.
Darn in ends.

chart 1

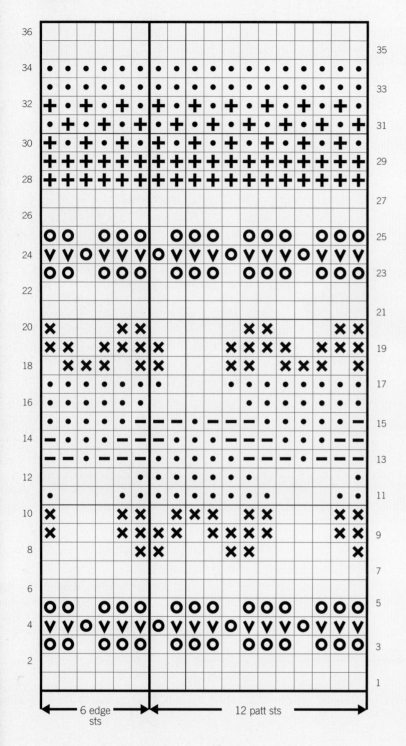

chart 2

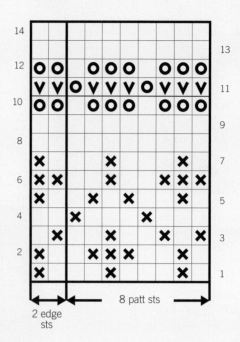

Note: fairisle chart 3 is on page 92.

	A
⊙	B
V	C
✕	D
•	E
—	F
✚	G

fairisle cuffs

These cuffs really do bring a traditional Fairisle design right up to date. They'll look great teamed with the Fairisle Legwarmers on pages 86–87 knitted in the same or a contrasting colourway. Quick and oh so simple to knit, they make a great gift for teenage girls and the young at heart.

measurements
Length: 10 cm (4 in)
Circumference: 15 cm (6 in)

materials
1 x 50 g ball Rowan Pure Wool DK in each of Clay 001 (A), Parsley 020 (B), Hay 014 (C), Marine 008 (D), Kiss 036 (E), Hydrangea 027 (F) and Glade 021 (G)
Pair of 3¼ mm (US 3) and 4 mm (US 6) knitting needles
Darning needle

tension
27 sts and 30 rows to 10 cm (4 in) over patt using 4 mm (US 6) needles.

abbreviations
See page 15.

note
■ Take care with the tension – if it's too tight the finished project will pucker.

cuffs
Using 3¼ mm (US 3) needles and A, cast on 42 sts.
Rib row: [K1, P1] to end.
Rep last row once more.
Beg at **. Work as Legwarmers (see page 86) until 26th row of Chart 1 has been completed.
Change to 3¼ mm (US 3) needles.
Rib 2 rows in A.
Cast off loosely.

to make up
Press according to instructions on yarn label.
With RS facing and using mattress st, join centre back seams.
Darn in ends.

fun & funky

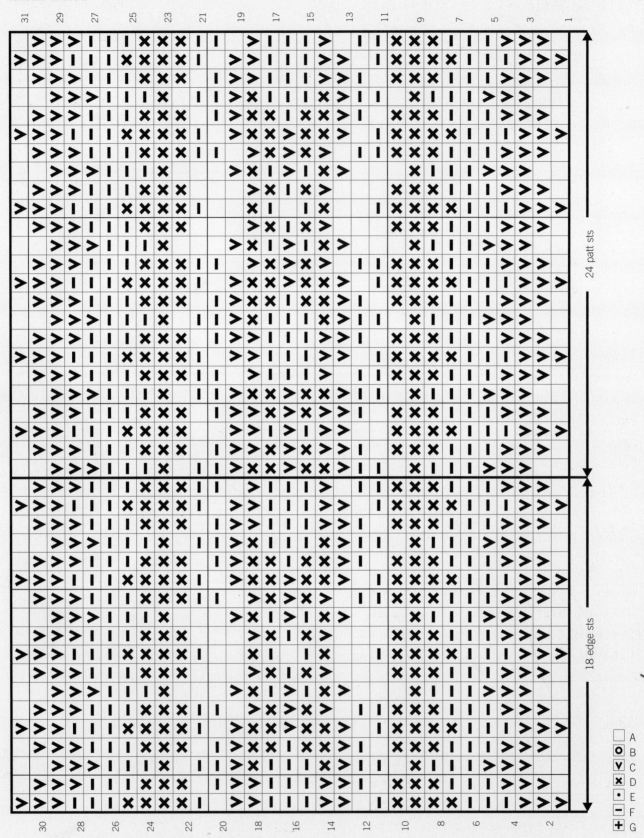

fun & funky

sideways gloves

The subtle colours of these gloves will suit any occasion, or why not create your own look and use several different shades. Great for using up oddments of DK yarn, you could try working numerous shades into each glove, or knit using black and white yarns to really make a statement.

glove

Work in g st throughout.

first piece

thumb

Using A, cast on 32 sts.

** **1st row:** K.

2nd row: K to last st, K into front and back of last st. (1 st inc)

3rd and 4th rows: As 1st and 2nd rows.

5th row: K.

6th row: K to last 2 sts, K2tog. (1 st dec)

7th and 8th rows: As 5th and 6th rows **.

shape thumb

9th row: K22, turn.

10th row: K to last 2 sts, K2tog.

11th row: K14, turn.

12th row: K4, cast off rem 10 sts.

1st finger

Join B to rem 21 sts, cast on 22 sts.

Work from ** to **.

Cast off 18 sts to complete 1st finger.

middle finger

Join C to rem 25 sts, cast on 20 sts.

Work from ** to **.

Cast off 20 sts to complete Middle

Finger.

ring finger

Join D to rem 25 sts, cast on 18 sts.

Work from ** to **.

Cast off 18 sts to complete Ring Finger.

little finger

Join E to rem 25 sts, cast on 14 sts.

Work from ** to **.

Cast off all sts.

second piece

thumb

Using 3¾ mm (US 5) needles, cast on 32 sts.

1st row: K.

2nd row: K into front and back of 1st st, K to end. (1 st inc)

3rd and 4th rows: As 1st and 2nd rows.

5th row: K.

6th row: K2tog, K to end. (1 st dec)

7th row: K.

8th row: K2tog, K21, turn.

9th row: K.

10th row: K2tog, K13, turn.

measurement
To fit average lady's hand

materials
1 x 50 g ball Rowan Wool Cotton in each of French Navy 909 (A), Misty 903 (B), Smalt 963 (C), Moonstone 961 (D) and Clear 941 (E)
Pair of 3¾ mm (US 5) knitting needles
Darning needle

tension
24 sts and 40 rows to 10 cm (4 in) measured over g st using 3¾ mm (US 5) needles.

abbreviations
See page 15.

notes
■ When sewing up oversew a few extra stitches between the fingers for strength.
■ Use ends of yarn to sew up gloves.

11th row: K.

12th row: Cast off 10 sts, K to end.

1st finger

1st row: Using B, K21, cast on 22 sts.

Work at First Piece from ** to **.

Next row: Cast off 18 sts, K to end.

middle finger

1st row: Using C, K25, cast on 20 sts.

Work as First Piece from ** to **.

Next row: Cast off 20 sts, K to end.

ring finger

1st row: Using D, K25, cast on 18 sts.

Work as First Piece from ** to **.

Next row: Cast off 18 sts, K to end.

little finger

1st row: Using E, K25, cast on 14 sts.

Work as First Piece from ** to **.

Cast off all sts.

to make up

With right sides together, sew all seams, leaving outer little finger side seam undone.

cuff

With RS facing and A, pick up and K 45 sts along wrist edge of glove.

K 7 rows.

Cast off in B.

Join rem seam.

Sew in all ends and press lightly.

Work 2nd glove to match.

Keep hands warm with these fun and practical gloves.

rosy bag

Summer days in country gardens, the sound of bees flitting among the flowers and the heady scent of cabbage roses as big as dinner plates are the inspiration for this pretty bag. Whether dressed up or keeping it casual, it's so gorgeous you'll want to take it anywhere and everywhere.

measurements

Depth: 27 cm (10½ in)
Circumference: 51 cm (20 in)

materials

1 x 50 g ball Rowan Pure Wool DK in each of Kiss 036 (A), Pomegranate 029 (B), Raspberry 028 (C), Port 037 (D), Tea Rose 025 (E), Parsley 020 (F), Emerald 022 (G), Glade 021 (H) and Enamel 013 (M)
Pair each of 4 mm (US 6) knitting needles
Two 3¾ mm (US 5) double pointed needles
1 m (1 yd) cord
2 large beads
Darning needle

tension

22 sts and 30 rows to 10 cm (4in) measured over st st using 4 mm (US 6) needles.

abbreviations

See page 15.

bag

Using 4 mm (US 6) needles and M, cast on 7 sts.

1st row: P.

2nd row (RS): K into front and back of each st. (14 sts)

Rep 1st and 2nd rows 3 times. (112 sts)

Beg with a P row st st 5 rows.

Cont in st st from chart reading odd-numbered (K) rows from right to left and even-numbered (P) rows from left to right. Use short lengths of yarn for each colour area, twisting yarns on WS at every colour change to link sts.

1st row (RS): K1M, patt 110 sts of 1st row of chart, K1M.

2nd row: P1M, patt 110 sts of 2nd row of chart, P1M.

Cont from chart in this way until 60th row of chart has been completed.

K 1 row M, P 1 row D.

Eyelet row: With D, K6, yf, K2tog, [K9, yf, K2tog] to last 5 sts, K5.

St st 2 rows each B, C and E.

Cast off M.

handle

Using double-pointed 3¾ mm (US 5) needles and M, cast on 6 sts.

1st row (RS): K6, do not turn, slide sts to beg of needle, pull yarn tightly across back of work.

Rep 1st row until handle measures 48 cm (19 in). Cast off.

to make up

Press according to instructions on yarn label. Join side seam. Darn in ends. On WS pin end of handle over side seam 2.5 cm (1 in) from top edge, pin other end opposite, sew both ends in place. Thread cord through eyelet row and knot a bead on each end.

rosy bag

110 sts

M
A
B
C
D
E
F
G
H

rosy cape

This beautiful cape will cheer up even the gloomiest of days and remind you of summer all year round. The pretty design suits all manner of occasions, from formal dinners to weekday shopping trips, and looks great with jeans. Throw it over any outfit for instant yet understated glamour.

cape

With 4 mm (US 6) needles and M, cast on 46 sts.

Cont in st st from chart using short lengths of yarn for each colour area, twisting yarns on WS at every colour change to link sts.

Cast on or inc at each end as shown on chart, read each row from left to right, then back from right to left.

On 60th row cast off centre 40 sts and complete each side separately, dec as shown and reversing chart for 2nd side to keep patt correct.

outer border

Using 3¾ mm (US 5) needles and M, cast on 6 sts.

Work in K1, P1 rib until border fits around outer edge. Cast off in rib. Sew in place.

inner border

Work as outer border until border will fit around neck and front edges. Cast off in rib. Sew in place.

to make up

Press according to imstructions on yarn label. Darn in ends. Cut ribbon in half. Take one length of each colour, gather ends and sew to corner, as shown. Attach ribbons to other corner.

measurements

Widest point: 70 cm (27½ in)
Length at centre back: 23 cm (9 in)

materials

2 x 50 g balls Rowan Pure Wool DK in Enamel 013 (M)
1 x 50 g ball Rowan Pure Wool DK in each of Raspberry 028 (A), Kiss 036 (B), Tea Rose 025 (C), Pomegranate 029 (D), Parsley 020 (E), Glade 021 (F) and Emerald 022 (G)
Pair each of 3¾ mm (US 5) and 4 mm (US 6) knitting needles
1.5 m (60 in) of satin ribbon in each of Pale Pink and Wine

abbreviations

See page 15.

tension

22 sts and 30 rows to 10 cm (4in) measured over st st using 4 mm (US 6) needles.

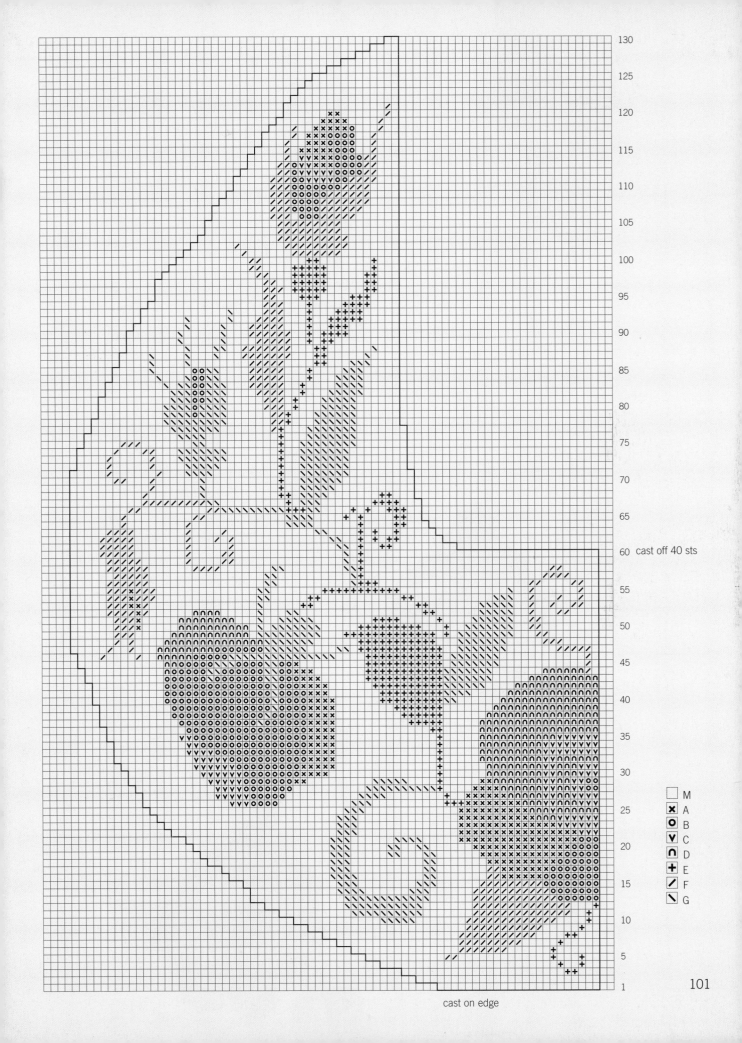

cast on edge

cast off 40 sts

	M
☒	A
◉	B
✓	C
∩	D
✚	E
╱	F
╲	G

flower pins

These flowers are so versatile and can be added to hats, slippers, bags or clothes. Be creative – use glitter yarn for an evening look or large needles and big chunky yarn for a dramatic flower pin for a coat. These ideas are merely a starting point, so go on and express yourself.

materials

Pair 3¾ mm (US 5) knitting needles
Darning needle

large flower

Colourway 1: small quantity Rowan Pure Wool DK in each of Damson 030 (A), Port 037 (B), Pomegranate 029 (C), Kiss 036 (D) and Emerald 022 (E).
Colourway 2: small quantity Rowan Pure Wool DK in each of Pomegranate 029 (A), Tea Rose 025 (B), Kiss 036 (C), Port 037 (D) and Avocado 019 (E)
Safety pin or brooch finding

flower bouquet

Small quantity Rowan Pure Wool DK in each of Kiss 036 (A), Tea Rose 025 (B), Pomegranate 029 (C) and Parsley 020 (D).
20 cm (8 in) floral wire
Safety pin or brooch finding

daisy and bead pin

Small quantity Rowan Pure Wool DK in each of Tea Rose 025 (A), Kiss 036 (B), Port 037 (C) and Pomegranate 029 (D).
Assorted beads of your choice
Beading thread
Large kilt pin

abbreviations

See page 15.

large flower

Using A, cast on 68 sts.
1st row: P. Change to B.
2nd row (RS): K2, * K1 and sl this st back onto left needle, lift next 8 sts, one by one, over this st, (yo) twice, K3, rep from * to end.
3rd row: K1, *P2tog, drop first yo, K into front, back, front and back of second yo, P1, rep from * to last st, K1. (38 sts)
4th and 5th rows: K. Change to C.
6th row: K.
7th row: K1, [K1, K2tog] 12 times, K1. (26 sts)
8th row: K1, [K1, K2tog] 8 times, K1. (18 sts)
9th row: [K2tog] 9 times, K1. (9 sts)
Cut yarn, thread through the rem 9 sts. Join seam. Darn in ends.

centre

Using D, cast on 2 sts.
1st row: K.
2nd row: Inc in first st, K1. (3 sts)
3rd row: K.

4th row: Inc in each of first 2 sts, K1. (5 sts).
5th row: K.
6th row: [K2tog] twice, K1. (3 sts)
7th row: K2tog, K1. (2 sts)
Cast off.
Sew in middle of Large Flower.

leaf

Using E, cast on 5 sts.
1st row (RS): K2, yf, K1, yf, K2. (7 sts)
2nd and every WS row: P.
3rd row: K3, yf, K1, yf, K3. (9 sts)
5th row: K4, yf, K1, yf, K4. (11 sts)
7th row: K1, K2tog tbl, K5, K2tog, K1. (9 sts)
9th row: K1, K2tog tbl, K3, K2tog, K1. (7 sts)
11th row: K1, K2tog tbl, K1, K2tog, K1. (5 sts)
13th row: K2tog tbl, K1, K2tog.
14th row: P2tog, P1.
15th row: K2tog tbl. Fasten off.
Sew to back of flower, as shown in photograph.
Sew pin to back of flower.

fun & funky

Be creative – use glitter yarn for an evening look and bright colours to add life to dark coats.

flower bouquet

flower

Make 2.

Using A, cast on 30 sts.

1st row: P.

2nd row: *K2, sl last st back onto left needle, lift next 4 sts, one by one, over this st, [yf] twice, K1, rep from * to end.

3rd row: K1, [drop first yf, K3] 5 times. Change to B.

4th row: [K2tog] 8 times.

5th row: [K2tog] 4 times.

Cut yarn, thread through rem 4 sts. Join seam.

Make another flower using C in place of A and A in place of B.

leaf

Make 2.

Using D, cast on 3 sts.

1st row: K1, yf, K1, yf, K1. (5 sts)

2nd and every WS row: P.

3rd row: K2, yf, K1, yf, K2. (7 sts)

5th row: K3, yf, K1, yf, K3. (9 sts)

7th row: K1, Ktog tbl, K3, K2tog, K1. (7 sts)

9th row: K1, K2tog tbl, K1, K2tog, K1. (5 sts)

11th row: K2tog tbl, K1, K2tog. (3 sts)

12th row: P2tog, P1. (2 sts)

13th row: K2tog. Fasten off.

Leave end to sew onto stalk.

to make up

Fold wire in half. From WS push one flower onto each end of wire. Beg at fold, wind D around both wires for 3 cm (1¼ in), then around one single wire to flower, wrap several times at the back of the flower to make it secure. Cut yarn and darn in end. Finish other side in the same way. Place leaves on stalks and wrap yarn ends firmly around stalk. Darn in ends. Wrap a short length of C around stalk and tie in a bow. Sew pin to WS.

daisy and bead pin

daisy

Using A, cast on 8 sts.

Work 8 rows st st.

Cast off.

Darn in ends.

Tie a length of A tightly around middle width, then tightly around middle length. Pull out each corner to form petals. Darn in ends.

Make another daisy using D.

Make one flower as given for Flower Bouquet, then make another using B in place of A and C in place of B.

to make up

Thread beads onto 2 lengths of beading thread making one length longer than the other. Missing the last bead of each length, thread back up through the beads again. Join daisy in A to one end of one length of beads and flower in A and B to other end.

Join daisy in D to end of second length of beads. Thread kilt pin through WS of flower in B and C, through daisy in D, then through second flower. You can also thread small charms, make tassels, tiny pompoms and keepsakes to customise your pin.

fun & funky

denim fingerless mitts

Always popular, denim cotton is easy to wear and is at home teamed with delicate floral frocks and country sweaters. Wash these gloves in the machine with your jeans and they will fade beautifully. Be creative and leave out the shaping to make wrist warmers.

measurements
To fit an average lady's hand

materials
1 x 50g ball Rowan Denim in Tennessee 231
Pair each of 3¾ mm (US 5) and 4 mm (US 6) knitting needles
Cable needle
2 stitch holders
Darning needle

tension
20 sts and 28 rows to 10 cm (4 in) measured over st st using 4 mm (US 6) needles.

abbreviations
See page 15.

note
■ The yarn used for this project will shrink a little when washed and the pattern allows for this.

right mitt
Using 3¾ mm (US 5) needles, cast on 46 sts.
P 2 rows, K 2 rows.
1st rib row (RS): K2, [P2, K2] to end.
2nd rib row: P2, [K2, P2] to end.
Rep last 2 rows until cuff measures 7 cm (2¾ in), ending with a 2nd rib row.
Change to 4 mm (US 6) needles.
Cont in cable patt for back and st st for palm **.
1st row (RS): K2, P2, [C4F – sl next 2 sts onto cable needle, hold at front, K2 then K2 from cable needle, K2, P2] 3 times, K18.
2nd row: P18, [K2, P6] 3 times, K2 P2.
3rd row: K2, P2, [K2, C4B – sl next 2 sts onto cable needle, hold at back, K2 then K2 from cable needle, P2] 3 times, K18.
4th row: As 2nd row.
Rep 1st to 4th rows once, then work 1st and 2nd rows again.
thumb shaping
1st row (RS): Patt 28, [inc in next st], twice, K16. (48 sts)
2nd row: P20, patt 28.

3rd row: Patt 28, inc in next st, K2, inc in next st, K16. (50 sts)
4th row: P22, patt 28.
5th row: Patt 28, inc in next st, K4, inc in next st, K16. (52 sts)
6th row: P24, patt 28.
Cont to inc 2 sts in this way, (working 2 sts more between incs), on next and foll 2 alt rows. (58 sts)
12th row: P30, patt 28.
13th row: Patt 28, inc in next st, K12, inc in next st, turn and leave rem 16 sts on a st holder.
14th row: P15, turn and leave rem 29 sts on a st holder.
*** Cont on these sts for thumb.
St st 2 rows.
P 1 row.
Cast off knitwise. Sew thumb seam.
*** With point towards thumb, sl 29 sts of back onto 4 mm (US 6) needle, pick up and K 1 st from base of thumb, K16 sts from st holder. (46 sts)
Next row: P18, patt 28.
With sts as set, patt 10 rows.
Next row (RS): Patt 28, [K4, inc in next st] twice, K3, inc in next st, K4. (49 sts) (Inc sts mark finger

positions.)

Next row: [P4, K1] twice, P5, K1, P5, patt 28.

Next row: Patt 28, [P5, K1] twice, P4, K1, P4.

Cast off knitwise.

to make up

Join side seam. Catching palm to back each time, sew finger positions from each inc to cast-off edge.

left mitt

Work as right mitt to **.

1st row (RS): K18, [P2, C4F, K2], 3 times, P2, K2.

2nd row: P2, K2, [P6, K2] 3 times, P18.

3rd row: K18, [P2, K2, C4B) 3 times, P2, K2.

4th row: As 2nd row.

Rep 1st to 4th rows once, then work 1st and 2nd rows again.

thumb shaping

1st row (RS): K15, [inc in next st] twice, K1, patt 28. (48 sts)

2nd row: Patt 28, P20.

3rd row: K15, inc in next st, K2, inc in next st, K1, patt 28. (50 sts)

4th row: Patt 28, P22.

5th row: K15, inc in next st, K4, inc in next st, K1, patt 28. (52 sts)

6th row: Patt 28, P24.

Cont to inc 2 sts in this way, (working 2 sts more between incs) on next and foll 2 alt rows. (58 sts)

12th row: Patt 28, P30.

13th row: K15, inc in next st, K12, inc in next st,

turn and leave rem 29 sts on a st holder.

14th row: P15, turn and leave rem 16 sts on a st holder.

Work as Right Mitt from *** to ***.

With point towards thumb, sl 16 sts from st holder back onto 4 mm (US 6) needle, pick up and K 1 st from base of thumb, K1, patt 28 sts from st holder. (46 sts).

Next row: Patt 28, P18.

With sts as set, patt 10 rows.

Next row (RS): [K3, inc in next st] twice, K4, inc in next st, K5, patt 28. (49 sts)

Next row: Patt 28, [P5, K1] twice, P4, K1, P4.

Next row: P4, K1, P4, [K1, P5] twice, patt 28.

Cast off knitwise.

to make up

As Right Mitt.

Wash these gloves in the machine with your jeans and they will fade beautifully.

suppliers

UK

The Knitting Parlour
12 Graham Road
Great Malvern
Worcester WR14 2HN
01684 892079
www.theknittingparlour.co.uk

John Lewis
Oxford Street
London W1A 1EX
020 7629 7711
www.johnlewis.com

Rowan
Green Lane Mill
Holmfirth
West Yorkshire HD9 2DX
01484 681881
www.knitrowan.com

US

Westminster Fibers Inc
165 Ledge Street
Nashua NH 03060
(603) 886 5041
www.westminsterfibers.com

AUSTRALIA

Australian Country Spinners
314 Albert Street
Brunswick
Victoria 3056
613 9380 3888
www.auspinners.com.au

SOUTH AFRICA

Arthur Bales PTY
62 4th Avenue
Linden 2104
27 118 882 401
arthurb@new.co.za

index

suppliers/index

acknowledgements

My heartfelt thanks to Chris Birch for helping with the knitting,
Emma Pattison for her calm patience, Sue Horan for checking my
hierglyphics, Paul Bricknell for the wonderful photography,
Susie Johns for the brilliant styling and Simon for being my best
accessory. Also grateful thanks to Rowan for keeping up
with my demands for yarn.